Sex Advent Calendar

Sex Advent Cupon

Day 1

Sex in the shower

 Sex Advent Cupon

Pick your fantasy

Sex Advent Cupon

Day 3

5 minute kiss

 Sex Advent Cupon

New position of your choice

 Sex Advent Cupon

Be my doctor

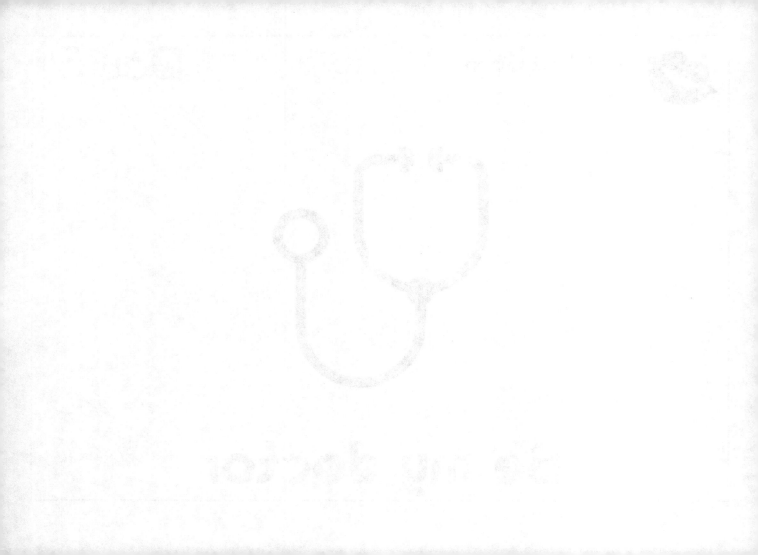

Sex Advent Cupon

69

Dress up

 Sex Advent Cupon

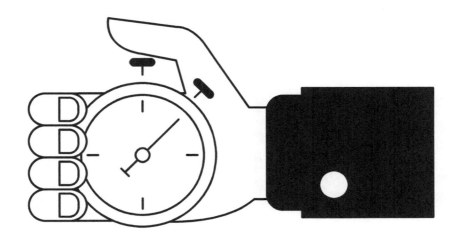

Quickie in an unusual place

Play with my ass

Sex Advent Cupon

Sex toy

Blindfolded sex

 Sex Advent Cupon

Serve dinner on my body

Be my sex slave for a day

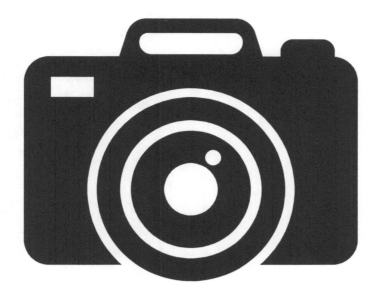

Erotic photoshoot

Sex Advent Cupon

Be my stripper tonight

Pussy licking day

Cassy licking dog

 Sex Advent Cupon

Early morning sex

 Sex Advent Cupon

Clean the house naked

 Sex Advent Cupon

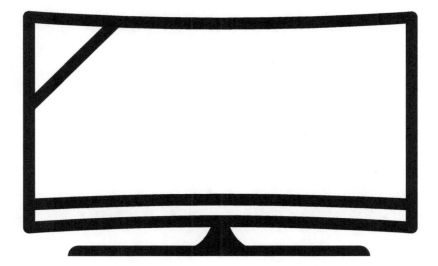

Let's watch porn

 Sex Advent Cupon

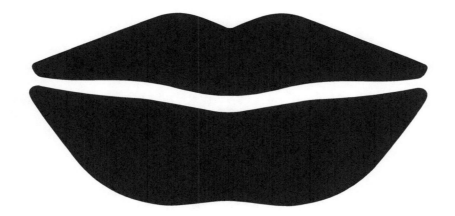

Get kisses anywhere you want

 Sex Advent Cupon

Middle of the night sex

 Sex Advent Cupon

Day of dirty texting

 Sex Advent Cupon

Blowjob day

 Sex Advent Cupon

Body massage